Lauren Carcara

P9-DYX-806

OTHER YEARLING BOOKS YOU WILL ENJOY:

THE MIDNIGHT HORSE, *Sid Fleischman*
SHILOH, *Phyllis Reynolds Naylor*
THE NOT-JUST-ANYBODY FAMILY, *Betsy Byars*
THE BLOSSOMS MEET THE VULTURE LADY, *Betsy Byars*
THE BLOSSOMS AND THE GREEN PHANTOM, *Betsy Byars*
A BLOSSOM PROMISE, *Betsy Byars*
WANTED . . . MUD BLOSSOM, *Betsy Byars*
BOBBY BASEBALL, *Robert Kimmel Smith*
MOSTLY MICHAEL, *Robert Kimmel Smith*
THE WAR WITH GRANDPA, *Robert Kimmel Smith*

YEARLING BOOKS/YOUNG YEARLINGS/YEARLING CLASSICS are designed especially to entertain and enlighten young people. Patricia Reilly Giff, consultant to this series, received her bachelor's degree from Marymount College and a master's degree in history from St. John's University. She holds a Professional Diploma in Reading and a Doctorate of Humane Letters from Hofstra University. She was a teacher and reading consultant for many years, and is the author of numerous books for young readers.

For a complete listing of all Yearling titles,
write to Dell Readers Service,
P.O. Box 1045, South Holland, IL 60473.

SID FLEISCHMAN

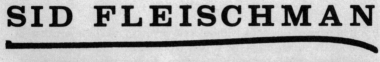

JIM UGLY

Illustrations by Jos. A. Smith

A Yearling Book

Published by
Dell Publishing
a division of
Bantam Doubleday Dell Publishing Group, Inc.
1540 Broadway
New York, New York 10036

ISBN: 0-440-40803-2

Reprinted by arrangement with William Morrow and Company, Inc., on behalf of Greenwillow Books

Printed in the United States of America

June 1993

10   9   8   7   6   5   4   3   2

For Jenna

Contents

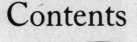

JIM UGLY

1

The Pine Box

I was hiding in the tall weeds. It was about the only place on the desert to hide from everybody. I remember when we first came to Blowfly, Nevada, my dad squinted one eye at the flat countryside and said, "Jake, I believe if you climbed a tree, you could see clear to Mexico. If you could find a tree."

I looked up at the hot, windy sky and watched a lone chicken hawk drifting like a speck of dust, hunting. Yesterday there had been a pair of them. I wondered what had happened to the other. Someone might have taken a shot at it. I wondered if birds of prey grieved.

I turned over and thought about what was going to happen to me and to Dad's dog, Jim Ugly.

Jim Ugly was a big sandy mongrel, part elkhound, part something else, and a large helping of short-eared timber wolf. There was wolf in his throat, too, for he never barked. He might yip or bay or wolf-howl, but mostly he was silent. I'd never seen such a quiet, keep-to-himself dog. You just never knew when he was going to behave like a dog or like a wolf.

Dad never got around to naming him. He had just called the dog Amigo, which means "friend" in Spanish, and sometimes Jim Amigo, but I never called him that. The mongrel never much liked me and I never much liked him, and out of spite I hung the name Jim Ugly on him.

He was a one-man dog—Dad's dog. And anytime I got too close to my father, there were Jim Ugly's yellow wolf eyes glaring like heat lightning.

Dad was buried less than a week ago, the morning of June 3, 1894. Jim Ugly was left to me, and me to Jim Ugly to get along as best we could. I'd hardly seen him since the funeral. He'd turn up once in a while, but mostly he kept to himself somewhere.

"If you won't shoot that infernal mutt, I will!"

It was my cousin Aurora, who was full grown, and her gambling man husband, Axie. She was always yelling that Axie was born tired and raised lazy, but I liked him. They were walking back toward the house and didn't know I was close by in the weeds. Dad and me had come to stay with them in Blowfly, where they were homesteading and Axie was growing about a million chickens. Who'd think to look for Dad on a chicken farm? He'd be safe.

Safe from that crazy yellowleg who was tracking him with a Colt army revolver. When I dreamed nightmares, I dreamed of the cavalry sergeant with the wide yellow stripes running down the sides of his blue pants. He couldn't still be in the army, not with a brown bowler hat cocked on his head, but he still wore his yellowleg pants stuffed into his boot tops.

After the funeral Aurora decided it was up to her to bring me up. But I just wanted to be left alone. I could bring myself up.

"He's the boy's dog now, Aurora," said Axie. "You can't shoot it."

"But that mongrel wolf is a sheep killer!" Aurora shouted.

"There's no proof."

"Ed Rippy saw him pull down a sheep, and he'll sue if we don't get rid of the mutt."

"Ed is a liar."

Aurora's voice had a lot of natural screech in it. "We can't keep a sheep-killing dog! I'll shoot the creature myself, Axie."

"Calm down. That dog's all your uncle left Jake."

"Except the diamonds."

"There are no diamonds, Aurora."

Someone in San Francisco had put a twenty-five-hundred-dollar bounty on Dad's head over some missing diamonds. "If I could find out who it was offering that money, I'd turn myself in and collect it myself," Dad had remarked in his rich, soft-edged voice.

At first the price on his head didn't seem to worry him. San Francisco was easy to stay out of. But not long after, we were crossing a muddy street in Monterey, where he had me in boarding school, and the yellowleg started blasting away at him. Dad shoved me down in the mud. In the yelling and confusion the bounty hunter disappeared.

A lead ball had lodged in Dad's right shoulder, but what made him so lightning-mad was that the yellowleg had come so close to shooting me. "Jake," he'd said, "pack your mother's picture, and let's make ourselves hard to find."

Not long after we settled in at Blowfly, the ball in his shoulder turned sore as a boil. He and Axie rode over to Smoketree Junction, where there was a doctor to dig it out. He wouldn't let me go along. He didn't want me any closer to him than necessary, not as long as that yellowleg was within a thousand miles. The morning he left was the last time I saw him.

Aurora was still carrying on about Jim Ugly. "That half-wild dog is apt to turn on *us* next. I'll shoot it tonight, after the boy's asleep, and he won't know it was me. Or care, if you ask me. There's no love lost between those two."

I heard the screen door screech open and bang shut, and their voices from the house faded away. I scrambled out of the weeds and around the barn where Axie kept his chickens. They made a constant noise, like a roomful of squeaky doors.

"Jim Ugly!" I called out.

He was nowhere about, but I thought I knew where he might have gone.

I walked to town and ended up at the cemetery, but he wasn't there either. I'd expected to find him at the grave, stretched out like the Sphinx and waiting for Dad to rise up and give him a whistle.

"Ain't seen that dog of yours," Mrs. Tribble told me. Her back porch looked out over all the headstones, and she couldn't help keeping an eye on things. "He just don't hang around here at all, Jake. Mr. Tribble was over in Smoketree Junction yesterday and said he saw him on the hotel porch."

I shrugged a little. How do you make a dog understand that someone just wasn't coming back anymore, and there was no point in looking for him in Smoketree Junction or anywhere else?

I was heading home when I caught sight of Jim Ugly on the road behind me, coming along at a steady wolf trot. Where had he been? Over in Smoketree Junction again? I picked up a stone and shied it at him.

"Jim Ugly!" I shouted. "Beat it! Git! You can't go home."

The stone raised a rusty blossom of dust where it landed in front of him. He didn't run. He didn't even flinch. He just looked at me as if I was a pesky boy standing between him and home and he'd wait until I got out of the way.

I heaved another stone and came close to hitting him. "Go on, Jim Ugly!" I called. "Tail it out of here! You won't find Dad at Aurora's, so stop looking! And folks won't abide a sheep-killing dog! It don't matter it you did it or not, as long as folks think you're a sheep killer. So clear out!"

I threw a clod of dirt that exploded on his shoulder and made him flinch. He danced off to one side, but only for a step or two. His small ears stood up sharp as tepees, and his eyes fixed me with a brooding, baffled stare. What was I bothering him for and standing in his way?

"Bust and run, unless you want to get shot!" I heaved another couple of dirt clods, hitting him both times. And then I turned my back on him, as if to let him know I wanted nothing more to do with him. I continued down the road. When I glanced back, he was sitting on his haunches, his tongue hanging out and his yellow eyes as sharp as stars. But when I glanced back again, he was following me at a wolf trot.

I figured he might be hungry, so I fed him on the back porch. Aurora threw a glance at us and smiled as if she hadn't anything more important on her mind than the pearl buttons she was sewing on a rustling green dress. She had about a dozen copies of *Godey's Lady's Book* and was always gazing moon-eyed at the latest styles.

"Jake, be careful that dog don't bite you," she said. "He's half savage, you know. You can't tell what a dog like that's thinking."

"Dad trusted him."

"You ain't your papa. I wouldn't turn my back to him."

"He don't bite."

And then she said, "Jake, look over those tombstones in the Sears, Roebuck catalog. I marked that six-dollar one in blue marble, guaranteed not to fade. But it's up to you to choose, Jake. They'll carve anything you want to say at two and a half cents a letter."

I tried to ignore the catalog split open on the table. My dad had been a newspaperman and an actor. I didn't think he wanted to be buried under a Sears, Roebuck tombstone.

"Jake, sure you never saw your papa burying a box or something around here?"

"Never," I said. She was at it again, asking questions.

"He never told you about a big bag of diamonds? Enough diamonds to hang the sky at night, someone told me."

Who would tell her a thing like that? It was just her imagination working.

"I could take care of you proper, Jake, if we were to find them diamonds," she said. "We could get out of this trifling, half-born place and away from those noisy, dim-witted chickens! They're driving me crazy! We could move to San Francisco, Jake, and ride around in carriages and raise a splash." Then she looked straight at me with eyes hot as branding irons. "Jake, your papa must have confided in you what he did with that confounded bunch of diamonds!"

"He never said a word, Aurora," I answered, and walked through the screen door to get one of my dad's shirts. I knew that Jim Ugly had a powerful fine nose. He had once slipped his rope and tracked Dad seven miles away over wet ground to a theater in Butte, Montana. Dad said rain freshened the scent, and it wasn't true a dog couldn't track through a river. The scent would float over the water like fog. He said Jim Ugly was a natural tracker, with a nose about a million times more powerful than ours. They spent a lot of time together practicing. "Jake, I believe Amigo could follow a three-week-old gravy stain on a man's vest clear to Los Angeles!"

I found one of my dad's long-armed checked shirts, and the touch of it filled me with a sharp longing. I felt the quick rise of tears. I forced them back. Swallowing hard, I ambled out behind the barn.

I held the shirt close to Jim Ugly's muzzle, and the scent seemed to shoot through him like lightning. He gave a small, anxious yip and pranced around on his big paws. He was acting like a dog, almost friendly, and looked at me as if I must be trying to say that Dad would be back any minute.

Axie came over with his hat brim pulled down almost to his eyes, the way he liked to wear it. "Jake, turn him loose," he said. "He'll be a dead dog by morning. He's a sheep killer."

"Coyotes about. It could have been coyotes."

"Most likely was, Jake. But the odds are against your dog."

"I'll run him off, Axie," I muttered.

"A half-wild dog like that can take care of himself," Axie said, and left.

I gave Jim Ugly another sniff of the shirt.

"Smell that?" I said. "Where's Dad? Think you can find him?"

I managed to get a long rope around his neck and tried again.

"Let's go!" I exclaimed.

Once he got the idea, he hoisted his tail like a kite. Off we went.

He practically dragged me all the way to town. But he didn't turn off to the burying ground.

I pointed to the headstones and called, "Over there!"

But Jim Ugly wouldn't even spare the place a glance. His nose was pulling him along the road, straight toward Smoketree Junction, where Dad had been killed.

I hauled up on the rope and pointed to the burying ground. "This way, Jim Ugly. Dad's in there."

Jim Ugly gave me a twitchy look, as if to say I didn't have enough brains to know my way outdoors without printed instructions. He turned his bushy tail on me and sniffed the reddish earth. There was no bird dog in him, but he might as well have been holding point straight toward Smoketree Junction.

My eyes tightened on the tombstones leaning up against the sunset. I knew for a sudden fact what Jim Ugly had known all along. My dad wasn't buried there. His scent wasn't on that rough, hammered-together coffin. The hair on my neck shot up.

Axie had lowered an empty box.

I sat down on the dirt, hunkering with my arms across my knees, and felt a wave of anger. Why hadn't Axie told me? The funeral was no more than show. What had happened to my dad over in Smoketree Junction? Where was he?

I jumped up, almost afraid to think what I was thinking. He could still be alive somewhere! And then I warned myself not to get all feverish about it, like Aurora and those perishing diamonds. I'd go slow, until I knew for sure one way or the other. It was clear to me that Axie wasn't going to tell me anything he didn't have to, but I'd head on home.

I slipped the rope off Jim Ugly's neck and turned him loose.

"Go on!" I bellowed. "Beat it! You can't follow me home. Don't you know what's good for you?"

Jim Ugly didn't look at me. He stood there staring off at the horizon. But he held his ground. I bellowed at him some more, but I knew I was wasting my breath. For all I knew, he was thinking that where I was, Dad was bound to turn up. He wasn't about to sashay out of there.

Not unless I ran off first. He might follow.

There was nothing much left in Blowfly to keep me. I turned the idea over in my head for a few steps and spit in the dust. I'd do it. I'd pick up a few things and be gone.

I slipped the rope back around Jim Ugly's neck and tied him to an old fence post.

"Wait here, Jim Ugly," I muttered. "If you think Dad's in Smoketree Junction, let's have a look. I reckon you've got the nose to find him."

2

I Run
Away

There was a buggy with wheels as yellow as daisies tied to the hitching post when I got back to the house. Voices trailed out from the parlor window, and I heard Aurora say, "You're a trifle late if you're trying to find my uncle. He's deceased, and I've only just stopped crying."

I could hear a man clear his throat. "Perhaps that was a different Bannock. The gentleman we're seeking is Samuel J. Bannock, a stage actor, formerly of Butte,

Cheyenne, Denver, and San Francisco. Is that your uncle?"

"That's him. Who are you, sir?"

"A loyal friend, ma'am. I am C. W. Cornelius of San Francisco, theater manager and producer of plays and extravaganzas. This lovely woman is the actress Wilhelmina Marlybone-Jenkins, the great stage star, whose career I manage."

Great stage star? I'd never heard of her.

"Sam Bannock's horse threw him over at Smoketree Junction," Axie said. "I had the pine box packed with ice for the trip home, and that's the way he was laid to rest."

"Cool and comfortable," Aurora added, and sighed loud enough to rattle the windows.

"It's true then!" the star cried out feebly, about ready to faint away.

I took a look through the blowing curtain and saw a lot of city clothes. The woman had a thunderhead of copper-colored hair, and she wore gloves to her elbows as if she'd dipped her arms in whitewash. She began to dab at her eyes with a handkerchief as thin and lacy as a handful of air.

"Sam Bannock gone to his reward!" she sobbed out to the second balcony. "Leaving me practically a widow!

Almost married—my lovely wedding dress nearly fills a closet! Now I'm left adrift in the world! My dear, beloved Sam! Snatched away in the midst of life—before I could wave him aloft. I shall wear black for the rest of my life!"

What was she hollering about! Almost a widow? Almost my stepmother! Not in a thousand years! Who was this woman sobbing up a flash flood? She was laying on the grief thick enough to plow.

"Control yourself, Wilhelmina," said the man, tapping a finger like a woodpecker at her shoulder. He had a big, red, beefy face with eyebrows like weeping willows. "Sir, would it be impertinent to ask if the departed left a will? Surely he named Wilhelmina Marlybone-Jenkins for a bequest. A few sparkling baubles perhaps."

"I should think not," put in Aurora, sounding cagey. "She didn't rate a mention."

The woman may have gone white for all I know; it was hard to tell under all the paint and powder.

"Everything went to the boy," Aurora added. "Not that my uncle left anything but a sheep-killing dog."

"A boy? What boy?" said the woman, her sharp nose rising out of the handkerchief as if she sniffed fire. "He never mentioned any *children* to me."

Well, he'd certainly never mentioned *her* to me!

"But he was always talking about Cousin Jake," said Aurora. "Maybe you just weren't listening, madam."

When the man cleared his throat, it sounded like someone moving furniture. "May I ask, was Sam Bannock seen digging somewhere on the property?"

"You must mean digging up potatoes and turnips," Axie replied, his face showing about as much expression as an acre of nothing. You could never be sure what he was thinking, and I reckoned that came from his being a gambler when he didn't have to feed and water the chickens.

"No, sir," said the man. "Possibly he was seen burying something for safekeeping."

"You mean the keg of diamonds?" Aurora exclaimed, fetching up an innocent smile. "Or was it a barrelful? Fairy tales! Nobody believes in that, sir!"

Wilhelmina Something-or-Other finished drying her eyes and put away the handkerchief. "Diamonds! Did you hear that, Mr. Cornelius? What an amusing notion! How *do* such absurd rumors get started?"

Aurora nodded, a wary look in her eyes. "Search me, madam. The first person I see around here with a pick and shovel will find we keep a shotgun handy." And then she added, as if they might know more than she did and be foolish enough to spill something, "Where would my uncle get a treasure of diamonds?"

"Where, indeed?" replied Mr. Cornelius, brushing aside his long eyebrows. "He stole them, madam. From us."

"I wouldn't believe that if it was printed on Bible paper!" Aurora screamed out. "The only thing my uncle ever stole was an hour's sleep! Axie, throw these city people out!"

"You must forgive Cornelius," Wilhelmina said quickly. "Theatrical managers have no manners. It's the first qualification for the job." And then she changed the subject. "Sam's darling boy—what did you say his name was? Frank? John? Elmer?"

"Jake," Aurora said sharply. "Jake Bannock."

"You know how boys are. Bursting with curiosity. How old did you say he was?"

"Twelve," Axie replied. "And no, madam, Jake hasn't shown the least curiosity in digging up the yard."

"Then perhaps," said Mr. Cornelius, tapping his lip, "perhaps the boy believes the treasure is lying elsewhere."

"You could be mistaken, Cornelius," Wilhelmina remarked. "I can't believe Sam would have light-fingered anything. I really must place flowers on poor Sam's grave and return to the hotel to weep in private."

"Quite right, quite right," said Mr. Cornelius. Then he added, turning to Aurora, "The lad hasn't run away, has he? Turned up missing?"

"Of course not. He and the dog have a home here."

"If he runs off, he'd be worth following."

"Why?" Aurora shot back.

"Sam may have told him where to dig. For the stones."

"For horsefeathers," Axie put in. "How do we know you ever owned a sack of diamonds? You'd need millions to buy them."

"No doubt," said Mr. Cornelius with a short smile. But he didn't offer to explain, and he didn't whip out a bill of sale.

I eased away from the window and dodged around to the barn. My dad stole diamonds worth heaps of millions of dollars? From them? Mr. Cornelius was lying! To start with, you'd have to be Queen Victoria or someone to own that many jewels! It was crazy. Everyone but Axie seemed to have gone light-headed over some phantom diamonds. They were even crazier if they thought I knew where Dad might have hid anything. Now if I told Aurora that I was running off, she'd want to go along with a pick and shovel.

I knew that in the night Aurora had dug holes under every corner of the barn, looking for the diamonds. It was a wonder she hadn't found the tin oyster can I'd buried not far off, under a feed sack.

I rattled my money out of the can, which seemed to scare the chickens into an uproar. There was $3.28 in silver and copper I'd earned at odd jobs during the last year or so. And there was a $5 gold piece my dad had given me. He'd have told me if he owned a treasure of diamonds, wouldn't he? The same as he'd have wanted me to know he'd about got himself a new wife. I didn't believe one, and I didn't believe the other.

It wouldn't do to have all those coins jingling in my pocket. I found a small rawhide sack to put them in. That's when I noticed Axie standing in the slanting light at the barn door.

"Did you drive the dog off?" he asked.

"About to," I said.

"He might be a sheep killer."

"Might be and is ain't the same thing."

"I know that, Jake. But when Aurora gets her mind made up, dynamite won't change it."

"Jim Ugly won't be easy to drive off. I may have to run him a long ways."

"Make sure he doesn't follow you back."

"Don't let Aurora get in a lather of sweat if I turn up missing for a while."

"I won't."

"Axie, you were with my dad in Smoketree Junction. You sure that was him you packed in ice for the trip here to Blowfly?"

"I nailed the lid down myself," Axie answered, and walked away.

I didn't know whether to believe Axie or not. If he was hiding something, you couldn't tell any more from his face than a stopped clock. I guessed that Dad had trusted Axie, but I was not sure that I should anymore.

I crossed to the house to get my coat and a pair of silver spurs Dad had given me. And my mother's locket and picture. It had been painted in New Orleans when Dad was on the *Picayune* newspaper. She was carried off in the cholera epidemic, and he quit the newspaper trade. He blamed his profession for bringing us to that "pestilential climate," as he called it.

I stared at the small picture. It was like looking at her through the wrong end of a telescope. But it was the only picture I had. I snapped the locket shut and shoved it in my shirt pocket.

There was no one in the kitchen, so I helped myself, throwing some leftover biscuits and dried plums in a flour sack and knotting the top. I could hear Aurora upstairs, yelling at Axie for wearing his hat in the house when they had company.

It was sundown when I returned to find Jim Ugly gone. You couldn't count on an uppity wolf. A dog would have waited, I thought. But Jim Ugly had gnawed through the rope. Well, I knew my way to Smoketree Junction without him. I picked up Dad's shirt and started out.

I don't think twenty minutes passed before I sensed that Jim Ugly was following me. Or following Dad's shirt. Night had fallen, but I could see his yellow eyes like two blinking stars in the dark.

He caught up, and I held the shirt bunched up in my hand for him to sniff again.

"Let's clear out, Jim Ugly. Smell that? Let's go. Let's follow that nose of yours."

3

Smoketree
Junction

S moketree Junction was a weedy scatter of buildings
on the railroad line. We were most of the next
morning getting there. Jim Ugly was generally out of
sight, far ahead of me in the sagebrush, with his nose in
the air and his tail wagging high.

He hardly spared me a glance except when the town
came into view about half a mile up the road. He finally
sat for a moment and gave me a lofty look, as if to say

I was a bother to have along. And did I have to make such a clatterwacking with my spurs?

The town dog, a bobtail mutt with stumpy legs, rose from the shade of a lacy green-pepper tree. He barked a warning as Jim Ugly approached, and it couldn't have been the first time. Cool as you please, Jim Ugly walked on by as if the other dog had never been born. The mutt lifted his lips to flash his fangs, but he just couldn't get Jim Ugly's attention. He snarled and charged, to make sure Jim Ugly knew who was boss around there. But some instinct told him not to nip in too close.

Wolves are chummier'n dogs, Dad told me, so the way Jim Ugly snubbed the town dog I reckoned must be the elkhound coming out in him. After a while the mutt quit barking and returned to the shade to nurse his hurt feelings. Jim Ugly just didn't feel the dog was worth the bother to lick. And he seemed to know exactly where he was going.

He hauled up at the Indian Princess Hotel, painted a barn blue, but peeling all over so that it looked like it was shedding its skin. Jim Ugly threw himself down in the shade of the porch, as if he'd been there before, and let his tongue hang out like a red bandanna.

This, I figured, is where my dad must have stayed to get the bullet pulled out of his shoulder. And then I read off the fancy letters in gold leaf in a corner windowpane:

EMIL FOSSUM, M.D. SECOND FLOOR.

I went up the polished wooden stairs. There was no need to knock. The door stood wide open.

Sitting in his shirtsleeves by the window and reading a newspaper, the doctor glanced at me over the tops of his glasses.

"You Jake Bannock?"

I stood for a moment, too astounded to answer. How had he come to know my name?

He broke into a laugh and stuck a cigar into his mouth.

"I saw that wolf of Sam Bannock's coming up the street and you following. I figured you might be Sam's boy come to find out exactly what happened here."

"Yes, sir."

"I don't know much, sonny."

"But didn't he come to get the lead ball out of his shoulder?"

"That's so," Dr. Fossum said. "I was digging around in his shoulder when he quick as lightning changed his mind."

"Was my cousin Axie with him? He didn't tell me about that."

"Axie? He was standing right here. Your father was gazing out the window when he suddenly reached out for his shirt and his hat. I hardly had time to yank the slug and tie up a bit of bandage. I figure he saw something from the window, and the two of them lit out."

I walked closer to the window and looked down. The only thing alive was a mule nibbling at the hitch rail of the barbershop. I couldn't see anything down there that would strike my father like a thunderbolt of lightning. But something had.

My eyes tightened on the orange depot, standing bright as sunset at the end of the street. "Maybe the train had got in."

"Seven minutes late," said Dr. Fossum, nodding. "Yes, I wondered about the train. If someone got off."

"Maybe it was a yellowleg in a bowler hat," I said.

"You mean D. D. Skeats?"

"Is that his name?"

"He got careless with his firearms the other night. I took some lead out of his foot. He claims to be a bounty hunter by trade."

"Is he still in Smoketree Junction?" I asked.

"I haven't seen him."

"He came looking for my dad."

Dr. Fossum struck a match to his cigar and puffed

27

away as if he were making smoke signals. "So he told me. He said he'd been to the funeral to show his respects."

"His respects? No, sir! No yellowleg showed up for the funeral."

"He was there," said Dr. Fossum. "He might have changed his duds and kept his distance, but he saw you and the dog and the preacher asking the Lord if he had a spare set of wings to hang on Sam Bannock."

It bothered me that the yellowleg had invited himself to the services. I reckoned he *might* have been there, for I hardly remember lifting my eyes from the ground.

Dr. Fossum said, "I thought your father might want the bullet to hang from his watch chain. I didn't have a chance to give it to him."

"Do you still have it, sir?"

"Think so."

He went over to a rolltop desk and rummaged through pill bottles and papers and held up somebody's gallstones in clear liquid for me to see. After a while he found a small medicine bottle with a lump of lead in it. "That must be it. A thirty-eight slug, as I recall."

I held it to the light for a moment and then jammed it into my pocket. I felt a tear start up, and I didn't want

it to show. "I'm grateful to have it," I said. "Dr. Fossum, do you know exactly how my dad died?"

"A horse threw him."

"That's what Axie said." Maybe it had happened that way, and maybe it hadn't. I didn't think there was a saddle horse born that could throw my father.

"Sir, I reckon you saw him laid out in his pine box."

"No," said Dr. Fossum. "I didn't attend the deceased. Nobody called me. The next thing I knew Axie had him on a wagon home."

I took a deep breath. "Could the undertaker have got the boxes mixed up? Maybe Axie brought the wrong one home."

The doctor slid his glasses lower on his nose and peered at me. "No one else died around here about then, sonny. There was no mistake."

I was smiling inside myself when I ambled back down the stairs. If the pine box Axie drove to Blowfly was just full of ice and empty as a gourd, then my dad might still be alive somewhere! I half believed it. I half didn't. I was afraid to get my hopes too perishing high.

I dropped down beside Jim Ugly on the porch. "Nice going, Jim Ugly!" I whispered, giving him a pat. I might as well have been patting a stone. "Maybe it was your nose that led you here, and maybe it wasn't. You could have remembered where Dad left you. I'm obliged to you anyhow, Jim Ugly. Put your nose to this."

I pulled the cork out of the medicine bottle and rolled out the slug of lead from Dad's shoulder.

Jim Ugly hardly seemed to breathe in the scent when he was up on all fours. He took another sniff, and I said, "Find him, Jim Ugly! Where's Dad?"

4
The
Travelers

Jim Ugly leaped off the porch, barely pausing to cast his nose about for the scent, and led me flying along the boardwalk. Once he had a smell in his nose, he followed it as if it was all a wonderful game to play. We passed the general store and the bakery and crossed the street toward the Smoketree Junction Bank. He hauled up at the stone step and seemed to lose the scent.

He seemed disappointed in himself and gave out a small whine. The town dog came trotting over to see what was going on. I think he wanted to wag his tail and get acquainted, but Jim Ugly wouldn't be sociable.

The next thing I knew he'd picked up the scent as if it hung like a mist along the side of the bank. He shot past the livery stable, and I lost sight of him behind a board fence.

I was making an awful racket with my spurs on, but no one bothered to give me more than a glance. When I caught a flash of Jim Ugly again, he was standing on the platform at the depot. He was looking around as if he expected Dad to be there.

So that was it, I thought. Dad must have caught a train out of town. Axie had lied to me and everyone else! I boiled over, thinking about it. Had Dad put him up to it? Didn't anybody think about me when they planned to lower that pine box full of ice into the ground? Or even Jim Ugly, giving his tail a wag if he heard a horse along the road, as if it might be Dad coming back? Axie could have told me the truth, even if he was just doing what my dad said. He could have trusted me!

"Nice going, Jim Ugly," I said when I caught up to him on the platform. I came close to giving his head a pat, but I didn't.

The stationmaster was polishing the brass telegraph

key with his pocket handkerchief when I stepped up. He was tall and thin and seemed to be mostly legs, like a sand crane.

"Sir," I said, "do you recall if Sam Bannock bought a ticket about a week ago?"

"Sam Bannock? I don't recall the name. He from around here?"

"Over in Blowfly."

"He the one got thrown by his horse?"

"Yes, sir," I replied.

"I didn't sell him a ticket to anywhere."

"Do you know Axie G. Hopper? Maybe he bought it."

"If Axie bought a ticket, I'd remember," said the stationmaster. "He didn't."

Dad could have climbed aboard without a ticket, I thought, and bought it from the conductor. Maybe he was being careful not to leave any more of a trail than he had to.

"What time does the train come through here?" I asked.

"Eastbound or westbound?"

That stopped me short. I couldn't guess which direction Dad might had gone.

"What's east?" I asked.

"Mostly desert and prospectors."

34

"What's west?"

"Mountains and prospectors."

It seemed to me that Dad had had enough of the desert.

The stationmaster pulled out his railroad watch. "The westbound is due in an hour and twenty-eight minutes."

"I'll buy a ticket."

"How far?" he asked.

"How far does it go?"

"Sunflower Creek, Red Sky, and Truckee."

"Just to the next town," I said, and counted out money for a ticket to Sunflower Creek.

"You'll have to keep your dog in the baggage car."

I was about to answer that Jim Ugly wasn't my dog but remembered that now he was. It was going to be some trouble getting used to.

"You'd better tie a muzzle on him. You got a piece of rope?"

"I left it behind. But he don't bite."

At least I didn't think he would. You couldn't be certain about a thing like that with Jim Ugly.

The stationmaster found an old piece of rope and slipped it across the counter to me. "The baggageman will be ever so grateful."

I waited on the platform for a while. I wasn't anxious

to tie Jim Ugly's jaws together. I felt a bit scared of even trying. I'd known him to snap, and he might bite over a thing like that.

He meandered off and drank out of the water trough, and I hoped he wouldn't decide to run off when the train came charging in. The town dog came closer with his tail wagging and howdy all over his face. It was as if he was trying to say, I've changed my mind, Jim Ugly, and you can be king of the street now. But Jim Ugly already knew that, and he meandered on back and curled up on the depot platform. That's when I tried to wrap the rope around his jaws.

He kept tossing his head so that I couldn't get the loop around. A look like a teased snake sprang into his eyes. My heart began to bang away. I didn't want him to see that I was afraid of him, so I went at it again. And he snapped at the side of my face. I got a loop around his jaws, but the next thing I knew, he had slipped out.

"Jim Ugly! Stop that! You're my dog now, and you might as well get used to it. Stand still, Jim Ugly!"

He glared at me, not a sound coming from his throat, not even a warning growl. We stood that way for a while, staring at each other, and I became aware of both

the stationmaster watching me and the town dog watching Jim Ugly.

"Stop acting so high and mighty," I said. "It's only an old ragged piece of rope. You've been roped before. I ain't enjoying this any more than you are. Now don't you move, Jim Ugly. Is that clear?"

I was afraid to try muzzling those teeth again. So I dropped the rope around his neck and made a loose knot.

"That's better," I said. "That's more like it."

I shot a glance at the stationmaster. "I'll ride the baggage car with him," I said. "And I'll keep the rope on him."

"That'll do," said the stationmaster.

I sat on the platform, and Jim Ugly curled up.

Before long I saw the wagon with the yellow wheels swinging into town. I watched as it drove up the street and into the livery barn. Mr. Cornelius and Wilhelmina came out on foot and crossed the street to the hotel.

The train was already in sight when they came sauntering toward the depot. Mr. Cornelius was burdened with three brown leather suitcases as brushed and polished as his shoes. Wilhelmina was carrying a white parasol with a breezy snowfall of lace around the edges.

For an instant I wanted to skip and run before they

recognized me. But then I realized that they had never seen me before. And they'd never laid eyes on Jim Ugly either. So I calmed myself down.

I saw her dabbing at tears with her handkerchief. They appeared to be real tears to me, and I heard her whisper hoarsely, "Poor Sam. Dear Sam. I cared about him so very much."

"Just do as I say, Wilhelmina."

I caught sight of the train way down the tracks, puffing up an advancing tornado of smoke. And suddenly Wilhelmina was beside me.

"Dear boy, you're bleeding!" she exclaimed. "You've hurt yourself."

She began dabbing at my ear with her handkerchief. Had Jim Ugly nipped me? He must have.

"Hold it there, child," she said, pressing my fingers to the handkerchief. It felt light as a cobweb. "How far are you going?"

"Sunflower Creek," I said.

"Have you ever been to the big city?"

I should have said no and let it go at that. But I couldn't let her think I was a purebred hayseed. "I've been to New Orleans," I said. "And even San Francisco."

I saw Mr. Cornelius look up at the mention of San

Francisco, and I wished I'd had better sense. But they didn't put two and two together.

"How wonderful," she said, but I could tell she thought I must be bragging and didn't believe me. "If you get back to San Francisco, you must come to the Mazeppa Theater as Mr. Cornelius's guest. He built it after the last fire."

I had sense enough now not to say that I'd been to the Mazeppa Theater once, when my dad had acted there in *Danton at the Bastille.*

"Cornelius, give this wounded child a complimentary ticket. How is your ear?"

"Fine," I said, and tried to give her the handkerchief back. It was kind of bloody, and she just smiled and told me to keep it. Had she really cared about my dad? I didn't know what to make of it.

The train came huffing in, raining sparks, and the conductor stepped down to help Wilhelmina and Mr. Cornelius aboard. I went forward to the baggage car. There was no way Jim Ugly could leap in while I held the short rope around his neck, so I let go. He jumped right on, and we settled ourselves near a shipment of wicker rocking chairs in the corner.

The baggagemaster looked over. "If that dog decides

to bite me," he said with a grin, "I aim to bite him back. Tell him that."

"Yes, sir," I said.

He slid the door of the baggage car shut. Before long the engineer let out a blast of steam, hit the bell, and we went rattling down the track.

5

Jim Ugly
Follows
His Nose

Jim Ugly curled up on the raw plank floor that creaked and shook under our feet. I gazed around at the trunks and suitcases and barrels and boxes, all ticketed and going somewhere, which was more than I could say for myself.

I looked at the baggagemaster, who had freckles as thick as rust spots. "How long to Sunflower Creek?" I asked.

He calculated it would be a mite over two hours, and

I wondered what I would do if Jim Ugly didn't pick up my dad's scent when we got there. I reckoned I'd buy a ticket to the next stop and keep going until my money ran out. But then what?

I shrugged and tried to stop thinking about it. I climbed up onto a packing box and watched out the window for a while. I began to count jackrabbits scared off by the engine and hightailing it through the sagebrush. But after a while I got tired of that.

It seemed to me my dad should have made sure I knew he was alive and fit. He shouldn't have let Axie keep the secret to himself. He shouldn't have played a trick like that on me.

The baggagemaster looked over from his swivel chair. "What you scowling about, kid?" he asked. "The look in your eyes is dark as tar. You and your dog ain't running away from home, are you?"

"No, sir," I answered quickly, not realizing I'd let my thoughts show. I must learn to keep my face from advertising everything, like Axie.

"I'd put you off this train if I thought you was running away."

"Truth is, I'm looking for my dad," I said. "It was him that ran off, but Jim Ugly here can track about anything. He's got the scent in his nose, and he's following it."

"To Sunflower Creek? That'll be worth seeing."

"If my dad got off there, Jim Ugly'll know."

I was surprised to hear myself make a brag dog out of him and eased off.

"Never heard of a name like that for a dog," said the baggagemaster.

"It suits him."

"A handsome dog like that?"

"He's not pure dog. He's part timber wolf."

"Looks friendly enough," said the baggagemaster.

"That's because you don't know him," I answered. "He's got a disposition about like barbed wire. He's no mongrel to brag about, no, sir."

The baggagemaster smiled as if he knew more than I did. "If he's a burden to you, boy, I'll be glad to buy him off you. What'll you take for him?"

Maybe I had begun to run down Jim Ugly more than necessary. "He's not my dog to sell," I answered. "And I'm counting on his nose if my dad isn't in Sunflower Creek."

When the train hauled up at the depot, the baggagemaster threw open the door. "We stop here only three minutes. Let's see what that wolf of yours can do."

I took hold of the rope around Jim Ugly's neck and gave him another close smell of the bullet.

"Find him, Jim Ugly!" I commanded, and off we jumped.

He lifted his nose and began plowing through the smells along the depot platform. He went back and forth, sniffing and panting, and finally I led him back along the tracks in case my dad had jumped off the train before it got to the depot. Through the window Wilhelmina caught sight of me and waved her fingers. I nodded and kept going, my spurs jingling.

But it was clear that Jim Ugly couldn't find the scent. The baggagemaster began flagging his arm and shouting at me, "Come on! You'll get left behind."

The engineer was already sounding the bell. I pointed to the baggage car, and Jim Ugly seemed content to jump back in. "I'll need a ticket to Red Sky."

"I'll let you ride free," said the baggagemaster. "It'll be worth it to see if that wolf of yours can do it."

The engine shot out great side-whiskers of steam. The baggagemaster gave me a hand up and slid the door shut.

I pulled off my spurs and stretched out. Jim Ugly slept most of the way to Red Sky. It was a water stop, high up in the foothills, and smelled of fresh-cut pine lumber. But that didn't appear to throw Jim Ugly's nose off. He rummaged about, sorting through all the different odors, and quickly tossed them aside.

"Dad ain't here, is he?" I muttered, and Jim Ugly turned his head to give me one of his pointy-eyed looks. There didn't appear to be much in Red Sky but the water tower and the sawmill, and I led Jim Ugly back.

"No luck?" asked the baggagemaster.

And I said, "Can't imagine my dad running off to a runty place like that."

"Truckee is bigger. It's growing up so fast I'm told they don't have enough bedbugs to go around. And if your dad ain't there, he likely laid over to change trains. Most folks do."

"They have a theater?"

"The Magnolia."

That gave me a little hope. Dad liked the company of actors. But for all I knew, he hadn't headed west at all. If he'd taken the eastbound train, I was scrambling in the wrong direction.

The train began to climb in earnest now, following a snail's trail of switchbacks until we must have risen a mile up the mountainside. The air was getting chillier the higher we climbed. When the engine pulled into the depot at Truckee, it seemed to gasp for air, blowing out thin, ragged drifts of steam.

I barely noticed Wilhelmina and Mr. Cornelius leave

the train, for once we hit the platform, Jim Ugly was off. It hardly took him a moment to pick up the scent, and I went bounding after him. I did turn back to see the baggagemaster give me a good-bye wave of the arm.

The town was across a wide, rutted street from the depot, and Jim Ugly crossed it as straight as if he were chasing a cat. He went loping along the boardwalk, pausing only a moment here and there to refresh himself with the scent, and turned up a side street.

When I caught sight of him again, I saw him scratching at the pine door of a shack sitting on tree stumps. My heart began to go like thunder. Jim Ugly was so anxious, I figured my dad must be on the other side of that door.

It flew open while I was still in the street. "What you scratching for? Beat it!"

It wasn't my dad.

It was the man in yellowleg trousers.

6

The Mistake

e gave Jim Ugly a kick with a bandaged foot and slammed the door. If he noticed me standing in the middle of the street, he didn't give any sign of it.

I knew in a flash that Doc Fossum had made a mistake. It wasn't Dad's bullet in the pill bottle. He'd given me the lead slug he'd dug out of the yellowleg's foot. That's who me and Jim Ugly had been following—the mangy, cuss-fired yellowleg! We hadn't been tracking my dad at all.

The door sprang open again. The yellowleg gazed at me with eyes like a flash of blue lightning. "What you staring at?"

"You, sir," I said quickly, figuring I'd better brazen it out. "I've never seen a yellowleg before."

"I usually charge admission," he said in a loud, blustery voice. His hair was short and matted like the fur of a dead cat. I was mostly afraid that he'd know me from my dad's funeral, but he didn't appear to remember.

"Is that pesky dog yours? Keep him away from here."

"Yes, sir."

He tightened up one eye. "Haven't I seen that bigfooted hound somewhere?"

"It wouldn't surprise me," I replied, and kind of held my breath at the same time. "He keeps to himself mostly, and I don't know where in tarnation he gets to."

That seemed to satisfy him, and he began to shut the door. But he stopped and caught me in his blue gaze again. I thought sure he recognized me now, even though I'd been dressed in my best clothes for the funeral, and my hair slicked down as wet as paint.

"What's your name, skinny?" he asked.

I didn't want him to know any more about me than necessary and hesitated.

"Don't you know your own name?" he said, and cracked a grin.

"Of course I do," I answered back. "And it isn't Skinny."

"I'm D. D. Skeats."

"Yes, sir," I said, but Dr. Fossum had already told me his name.

"Maybe you heard of me."

"I don't much see the newspapers," I said.

"I'm a bounty hunter. I catch people."

"Yes, sir."

"And I'm looking for someone."

"Here in Truckee?" Thoughts began to whirlwind around in my head. Hadn't he been fooled by Axie's playacting in lowering a pine box full of ice? Was he still after the bounty on Dad's head?

"You can save me a stroll on this game leg," he said.

"Someone shoot you?"

His head took a suspicious tilt. "How do you know I was shot, boy?"

The hair stiffened like quills on my neck. Where was my head, letting my mouth run loose that way? Then I saw his empty boot sitting on the floor inside the door.

"That looks like a bullet hole in the top of your boot,"
I said. "I figured someone may have shot you."

"No one's ever got the drop on D. D. Skeats," he said,
and eased off into a rumbling big laugh. "Did it myself,
boy. Tripped and shot myself in the foot!"

I don't know if he expected me to laugh with him or
not, but I kept a straight face. And Jim Ugly had lost
interest in him entirely, wandering away up the street.

"You go on back to Front Street," he said, "and I'll
pay you a dime or two. I heard the train just pull in. Go
around to the hotels. Spy out who checked in, and let
me know."

I felt a lump in my throat and tried to swallow it.
"Whose name are you looking for?"

"A woman named Wilhelmina Marlybone-Jenkins."

I almost broke into a smile of huge relief but didn't.
It wasn't my dad he was bounty hunting, so I reckoned
Axie had fooled him after all. But why Wilhelmina
What's-Her-Name? Was she on his bounty list?

I didn't intend to run his errands. But I said I would.
There'd be no harm in warning Wilhelmina before he
stirred.

"Here's a dime now, and the other when you get
back."

"No, sir," I said. I wouldn't take money from a man

who'd put a lead ball in Dad's shoulder, not in a million years. "No charge."

I ran off, not intending to come back. But Jim Ugly wasn't following me. I trudged back up the street and got him by the rope collar and led him away. The yellowleg stood in his doorway, watching me.

"I'd swear I know that dog from somewhere," he said.

7

I Meet Mrs. William Tell

I wanted to tell Jim Ugly it wasn't his fault we'd ended up in the wrong town. And I started to, but he loped away with his nose to some deer tracks that interested him more than the sound of my voice. He wasn't going to stick to my legs as if I owned him.

It didn't take long to track down Wilhelmina. She and Mr. Cornelius had taken rooms at the Webber House. But neither of them was in.

When I came back outside, I looked around for Jim Ugly. I figured he must be hungry, and I ought to get him something to eat. I tried whistling for him, but if he heard me, he didn't come running.

I decided to look in on the Magnolia Theater. They might know an actor named Sam Bannock. They might even have seen him if he'd been in Truckee to change trains. I let myself hope that he had touched something in the theater so that Jim Ugly could pick up his scent again. But I knew better than to count on anything.

The posters out front said:

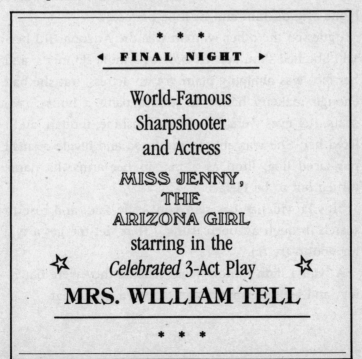

* * *

◀ **FINAL NIGHT** ▶

World-Famous
Sharpshooter
and Actress

**MISS JENNY,
THE
ARIZONA GIRL**
starring in the
☆ *Celebrated* 3-Act Play ☆
MRS. WILLIAM TELL

* * *

There was no one to keep me out, so I walked into the darkened theater. There wasn't a soul on the stage, but I soon heard voices from a dressing room full of trunks and props and costumes. And there sat Wilhelmina and Mr. Cornelius drinking tea out of little cups with a large woman in pointed red boots and a velvet jacket.

Wilhelmina's face glowed up when she saw me. Her arm made a vast sweeping gesture as if to accompany a blare of trumpets.

"There he is!" she exclaimed. "Jenny, dear, put a blond wig on him and he'll be perfect."

I guessed the other woman was the Arizona Girl herself. She had shoulders as wide as a mule skinner's, and her face was almighty plain, for an actress, but she had enough makeup handy in jars to paint a house, two coats. Her eyes were friendly as sunshine, though, and I liked her. She was able to drink tea and juggle a small pug-faced dog, limp as a rag, in her arms. Its name turned out to be Pieface.

"It's Providence has sent you!" she said, and rose to search through an open trunk. "Here, let me get a wig for you to try on."

A wig? I didn't know what scheme they were hatching, and I didn't much care. I cleared my throat.

"Miss Wilhelmina Marlybone-Jenkins?"

"On occasion," she answered with a smile, and I figured that must be her stage name. "Come here, child. Would you like to be an actor?"

"No," I murmured.

And then I lowered my voice another notch or two. "I came with a message for you."

"Don't bother me with trifling messages. How would you like to play William Tell's son?"

So that was what they wanted me for! I was born with better sense. "And have an apple shot off my head?"

"But this is Miss Jenny, the famous sharpshooter. It'll be safer than walking down the street."

"Just for tonight's performance," said the Arizona Girl, hauling a blond wig into the air as if it were a dead chicken.

"The boy in the company has suddenly retired from the theater," explained Mr. Cornelius.

Miss Jenny threw her dog over one shoulder and began brushing out the blond curls. "Poor boy," she remarked. "Young Ellis tried to climb a dead granddaddy of a hollow old cedar tree south of town. But what does a city boy know about country matters? A family of skunks was homesteading that hollow tree. Young Ellis just about cleared out the theater last night."

"How thoroughly unprofessional of him," snapped Wilhelmina.

"The boy's mother will be scrubbing him for a week," added the Arizona Girl with sympathy.

I was sorry about the boy with the skunk, but I had more than enough troubles of my own. "Miss Marlybone-Jenkins," I said, "it's *not* a trifling message. I came to tell you there's a man looking for you."

"In Truckee? Not a soul knows I'm here, darling child."

"A mysterious message?" said Mr. Cornelius, putting down his teacup without a sound. "It doesn't surprise me. That could only be Sam Bannock."

"Sam Bannock!" she exclaimed, and turned to the markswoman. "Jenny, have you seen him? The actor! Is he here in Truckee?"

"Wilhelmina, I haven't seen anyone in town who can act, including my leading man."

Mr. Cornelius narrowed one eye. "I tell you that funeral of his was a stage trick. It was altogether too convenient. And too much like the graveyard scene in *The Huddlestone Ghost*."

"Act one, scene three," said Wilhelmina, who suddenly declaimed as if the footlights were ablaze before her. "'*Rise up, bloody bones, and shake yourself!*' Sam was dashing as Huddlestone."

"Don't forget he sent you an urgent letter to come to that vile little grease spot in the desert," said Mr. Cornelius. And then he added, with a scoff, "He wanted to be sure he had an audience when the curtain fell."

"Then he should have held the curtain until we arrived."

I must have been gazing at her in amazement, but no one seemed to notice. She had come to Blowfly at Dad's invitation? Why? Couldn't he have trusted me enough to mention her name?

"It wasn't Sam Bannock," I said.

Her eyes brought me back into focus. She appeared crestfallen. "Not Sam Bannock? Who are you, child? Who sent you?"

"It was a bounty hunter, miss."

"I don't know any bounty hunters!" she declared flatly.

"But he knows you," I said. "If there's a reward on your head, he means to collect it."

"A bounty on the head of Wilhelmina Marlybone-Jenkins?" She burst into a short laugh. "For what? Giving a bad performance? That, my child, is not yet against the law."

"What does this bounty hunter look like?" Mr. Cornelius asked.

"He's big enough for two," I said. "He's got eyes that hardly blink. He just stares at you. And he shot himself in the foot."

"A perfect stranger to me," Wilhelmina exclaimed impatiently.

I went on. "He was a yellowleg soldier and still favors the pants. His hair is matted down as if he uses a lot of bear grease on it."

A change came over Wilhelmina. Her eyes seemed to dim. She looked at Mr. Cornelius and then back at me. "Would his name be D. D. Skeats?"

"So he said."

Wilhelmina put down her teacup as delicately as if it were an eggshell. "What could that unwashed ruffian want with me?"

Mr. Cornelius said, "Perhaps he thinks you can lead him to the elusive Mr. Bannock."

"All I want to do when I find the elusive Mr. Bannock is to horsewhip him." She bristled, and her eyes flashed at the Arizona Girl. "An affair of the heart, Jenny."

"I've heard."

They rattled on as if I were only another empty costume hanging on the dressing room door. It didn't occur to them that I was understanding a lot of what they said.

"Isn't there a train out of here earlier than tomorrow?" Wilhelmina asked, as if she were all for pulling a vanishing act. "Are we stuck in Truckee?"

"It appears that we are," said Mr. Cornelius.

"You're an actress, dear Wilhelmina!" declared the Arizona Girl. "We can make you over in this dressing room so that the man will never recognize you."

"No," said Wilhelmina. "I'll face up to the bounty hunter and tell him I won't be followed. I'll tell him that he's a fool, an idiot, and a distinct nuisance."

"But he can be quite dangerous," Mr. Cornelius reminded her.

She dismissed the warning with a flick of her hand. "Don't be tiresome. You do get on one's nerves, Cornelius." She asked Miss Jenny for a scrap of paper and an envelope and wrote out a message at a full gallop. Then she handed it to me.

"Be so good as to deliver this to the yellowleg person with bear grease on his hair," she said. "And then rush right back. Jenny will need to rehearse you for this evening's performance."

Fearless
and
Defiant

I had no intention of returning to put on a wig and
have an apple shot off my head. I looked around for
Jim Ugly. There were wagons going by, and the baggagemaster came sauntering up the street, but Jim Ugly
was nowhere in sight.

I wasn't anxious to meet the yellowleg face-to-face
again, but I felt obliged to deliver Wilhelmina's message.
I didn't want to like her. But it was getting kind of hard
not to like her.

I knocked on the door of the yellowleg's cabin. He didn't answer, and that suited me fine. I hoped to be far away before he recollected where he'd seen Jim Ugly. Once he realized it had been Dad's dog scratching at his door, and me trailing along behind, he'd have sense enough to know there was something peculiar in the wind.

I slipped the message under the door and took off down the hill. There was nothing left to keep me in Truckee, except that I didn't have a notion where to go or how to get there.

I began meandering along the boardwalk, my hands jammed in my pockets, when a thought went through me like a flash of sunlight. *Wilhelmina had received a letter from Dad's own hand!* Maybe she had it with her. If Jim Ugly could pick up Dad's scent again, he might be able to point me in the right direction.

The smell of fresh bread stopped me in my tracks, and I gazed through the bakery window. I'd forgotten how hungry I was getting. I went inside and counted out some pennies for a nickel's worth of gingersnaps.

It was then, through the window, that I saw Jim Ugly across the railroad tracks. He was striding along the riverbank as if being chased by hornets. Only it was the yellowleg chasing him. He was riding a burro, whipping it to a trot, with his long legs all but scraping the ground.

My mouth full of gingersnaps, I lit out as if I'd been shot from a cannon. I knew that Jim Ugly must have stirred the yellowleg's memory. The bounty hunter had pulled a boot over his sore foot, picked up a rope, mounted a burro, and gone out searching for a closer look.

I was out in the middle of the street when I put on the brakes. What was I going to do—flag my arms and try to whistle Jim Ugly to me? I didn't have good sense. Why make it easier for the yellowleg to put me and Jim Ugly together? No one was going to catch that dog. I'd keep myself scarce.

I watched Jim Ugly racing off. You'd think he was running for the live joy of it. After a moment the yellowleg gave up the chase and sat for a moment, thinking. Then he swung the reins across the burro's neck, and they began crossing the railroad tracks.

I ducked well out of sight around a freight wagon loaded with stovepipes. The yellowleg had hardly crossed at the corner when out of nowhere Jim Ugly came up behind me. I supposed he could follow my scent anytime he felt like it.

He plopped down on the ground to catch his breath, and I glared at him. "Don't look so pleased with yourself," I muttered. "That yellowleg must be suspicious. How am I going to hide you from him? Tie you up somewhere?"

He was still wearing the short loop of rope I'd slipped over his neck, and I took hold of it. Tie him up where? And then what? I could count on the wolf coming out in him the moment he found himself at the end of a rope. He'd start a howling rumpus.

In hardly any time at all I found myself heading back to the theater with Jim Ugly in tow. I knew what to do. There were all those jars of stage makeup. I'd try turning Jim Ugly into a spotted dog or something.

I stopped on the way and got some meat scraps at the butcher. Once inside the theater door, I opened the butcher paper and left Jim Ugly there to eat.

"I'll pay you seventy-five cents per show," the Arizona Girl said, trying the blond wig on me and hanging on to her dog at the same time. Then she put a green apple on top of the wig. "Balance it, young feller. Walk around to get used to the feel of it."

Seventy-five cents all at once seemed a huge sum, but I had no intention of showing up for the evening performance. All I wanted was to see what I could do with Jim Ugly. "Not much money to risk my neck," I said.

She gushed out a laugh and gave me a wink with her left eye. "Follow me."

She led me behind the front curtain. A forest of painted trees, looking as flimsy as paper dolls, filled the stage. It wouldn't have surprised me to see my dad step out of the woods, fix me with one eye, and take a bow.

The apple dropped off my head a couple of times, but she seemed to expect it. Then she showed me the place I was to stand against a tree, and if she hadn't stopped me, I'd have walked into the plate glass in front of it.

"The audience never sees it. I've never missed the apple yet, child, but only a scrambly-witted fool would take a chance like that. You mustn't tell a soul about the glass."

"Not anybody," I swore, with considerable relief. The seventy-five-cent salary began to tempt me. I'd need every cent if I was going to keep me and Jim Ugly fed and on our own.

"What about your mother?"

"All I've got left is a picture," I answered. I came close to hauling it out to show to her, but I didn't.

"An orphan?"

I hesitated. I didn't know what the right answer was.

I'd never before thought of myself as an orphan, and I might not be! But it seemed simpler to nod, so I nodded.

She told me that this version of the play had been written especially for her. William Tell is so worried he takes to drink, and his hands shake. Mrs. William Tell, played by the Arizona Girl, the famous markswoman, puts on a red beard and pretends to be her husband when he's forced to shoot an apple off his own son's head.

My part was easy. I was only onstage a few minutes, but I was supposed to hold a fearless and defiant look in my eyes.

"The curtain rises at eight tonight," she said. But I was to be there by seven-thirty to get into my costume.

She surprised me by paying me the seventy-five cents in advance, and I looked up into her smile. She was counting on me. I looked at the coins and then closed my hand on them. I felt a part of her theater company. I smiled back.

She had to leave, and I said I wanted to stay behind to practice looking fearless and defiant. I also told her I had a dog out front.

"I hope he won't bark during the performance!"

"Not a chance of it," I assured her, and she left.

I got a hand on the short rope around Jim Ugly's neck

and led him down the theater aisle. He resisted some, but just out of habit, I think, for he came along and I got him to the dressing room.

"Now stand still," I commanded. I unknotted the rope, and meant to keep it off, for the yellowleg was bound to have noticed it.

I studied Jim Ugly's fur, and for the first time I saw how many colors he had. His muzzle was honey-colored with flecks of gray, and there were hairs along his back as orange as marmalade. I picked up a fancy tin box of rice powder and used the puff to blot out the orange.

I don't know what Jim Ugly was thinking, but it surprised me that he was so patient about it. He hardly flinched when I got a burnt cork out of the glass jar and darkened his ears and the end of his tail. And then I recalled that Dad had often kept him in his dressing room and that these smells would be nothing new.

I studied him and then went back to the rice powder. He ended up mostly a dirty white, but he looked different enough to suit me.

Then I practiced making faces in the mirror. Finally I turned to Jim Ugly and lifted one eyebrow.

"Do I look fearless and defiant?"

9

The
Letter

I had a picture in my mind of Dad's letter to Wilhelmina folded inside the sparkly bead-covered purse she carried. Or did she have it laid away in one of her suitcases? I shrugged off the notion that she might have thrown it away.

Jim Ugly would need a sniff or two of that letter to track Dad's scent. But how was I to get hold of it? Wilhelmina wasn't apt to hand it over to a stranger. "Of course, child! Of course, you can read my personal mail, whatever your name is."

Not in a thousand years! Suddenly Dad's voice came to me as if he had stepped to the footlights. "Be bold, Jake! 'Boldness, again boldness, and ever boldness!'" *Danton at the Bastille*, act two, scene three.

I'd try.

Jim Ugly shook himself and raised a cloud of rice powder. Once outside, he went bouncing around in the brisk air, and I hardly recognized him myself.

"Heel!" I commanded. He knew what it meant, but it didn't interest him to heel for me. He flashed me a short glance as if to say I couldn't possibly be going anywhere that interested him. I set out for the hotel alone.

In the lobby I saw a couple of men in capes and cravats and stickpins with stones the size of glass paperweights. I had a notion they were actors. William Tell himself sat in a leather chair, reading a newspaper. I recognized him from the theater posters. I guessed the whole company of players must be putting up at the Webber House.

I'd already devised my speech by the time I knocked on Wilhelmina's door and rehearsed it while I waited for her to open it.

When she appeared, all copper hair and a surprised smile, I forged ahead boldly. "Miss Wilhelmina Marlybone-Jenkins," I said. "I know the yellowleg gent to be a desperate character. He put a bullet in Sam Bannock's shoulder. If there's a letter from Sam Bannock, it's bound to say it was D. D. Skeats who tried to murder him in cold blood. That yellowleg would as soon shoot you for it as not."

Her eyes opened up like the petals of a four o'clock. I seemed to be taking her breath away.

"He's that mean," I rushed on. "His hide's full to the top with meanness. I could slip that letter in my back pocket for you. It'd be safe there if he was to rip open your purse."

"I wouldn't want to trouble you," she said at last.

"No trouble at all, miss."

"But the letter didn't say anything about D. D. Skeats shooting at him."

"He'd think it. Bound to."

"Let's not worry about the yellowleg," she said, and it was clear she wasn't taking me very seriously. "As for the letter, it's not in my purse."

"I guess it wouldn't be," I said, thinking as fast as I could. "Well, of course not," I went on. "A thing like that belongs in a suitcase."

"No, young man," she answered. "I left it in San Francisco with my other love letters."

I felt the air go out of my boldness. Love letters? Is that what Dad had written her? A tarnatious love letter? I tried not to let confusion show on my face, but I suppose it did.

"I don't suppose you've got anything else of his hanging about?" I muttered softly.

"Nothing," she answered. The way her eyes fixed themselves on me, I knew she was trying to read my mind. "Why are you so interested in Sam Bannock?"

"I heard you talking about him."

"I didn't say anything about a bullet in his shoulder. Who are you?"

"Me, miss?"

"What's your name?"

"My stage name, you mean?"

She didn't give me time to think of one. She didn't need to. She already had me added up like a sum of numbers. "You're that boy of Sam Bannock's, aren't you? John?"

"No," I answered after a moment. "Jake."

She took a small breath and began to smile. "I'm glad to know you at last, Jake. Call me Wilhelmina. Come in."

She motioned me to a rocking chair at one window

and then stood as straight as a parasol at the other.

"Sam didn't tell me about you," she said, as if it were my fault.

"He didn't tell me about you either," I said.

"A gentleman doesn't bandy about a lady's name," she answered, snapping to his defense. Her chin was tilted, and her eyes were fearless and defiant.

She has it down exactly right, I thought. I'd try to do it that way myself tonight.

There was a dead silence, and through the window I watched heavy clouds breaking like ocean waves over the hilltop. I hoped it wouldn't rain. That would wash out Jim Ugly's disguise.

"My dad didn't steal your diamonds," I said firmly.

"Of course, he didn't."

"Then why is Mr. Cornelius after him?"

"Because Mr. Cornelius disagrees. Mr. Cornelius is convinced that Sam has forty pounds of diamonds. Forty pounds! Can you imagine that?"

"No."

"And I must own a pound or two! Cornelius, who manages my business affairs, has confessed to me that he used my money to help buy the sparkling hoard. I much prefer stage jewelry. The stones are so much bigger! But off he went to Amsterdam to buy diamonds in bargain lots and was then careless enough to allow them to be stolen."

"Maybe the police will find them, or something."

"He refuses to notify the police!"

"Why?"

"Perhaps there's something fishy about those diamonds." She lowered her voice to a whisper and grinned. "Perhaps he smuggled them into the country. Imagine!"

"My dad didn't take them!"

"I promised to help Mr. Cornelius find the diamonds. He promised to help me find your father. Maybe if those two meet, they can settle their misunderstanding. And someone will call off that yellowleg assassin!"

My spirits lifted, but only for a moment.

"So, Jake, if you've come to Truckee to meet your father, trust me. Tell me where you are meeting."

My guard shot back up. "You've got it wrong," I said. "My dad is not in Truckee."

I got up. I saw it start to rain and began to worry about Jim Ugly. "I'll be going."

She held out her hand, and I shook it quickly. The bones in her fingers seemed hardly bigger than a bird's.

"Good luck tonight," she said. "I'll be in the audience to applaud your fearless performance." And then she added, "Let's keep an eye out for Sam Bannock. He can smell greasepaint and stage dust miles off—wherever he is."

10

Bared Fangs

The rain came tumbling in, catching some men in the street, and pouring like molten silver off their hats. I cast a glance for Jim Ugly. He'd probably sheltered himself somewhere.

I kept to the covered boardwalk. When I turned the corner, there was Jim Ugly way up the street. The rice powder was running off his fur like whitewash.

Confounded mutt! Any dog would have sense enough

to climb under something. But the wolf in Jim Ugly wouldn't step out of the way of a downpour of rain.

I hurried closer, keeping to the covered walk. I was about to call out when I felt myself lifted off my feet. Someone had me by the back of the collar.

"You know that dog, don't you?"

I knew the yellowleg's voice. My hair stiffened. He swung me about as if I were hanging in a noose. I found myself looking into his eyes, deep and black as caves.

"He your dog?"

"No, sir," I said. That was close enough to the truth, for Jim Ugly still felt like Dad's dog.

"You were about to call to him."

"He appeared to be drowning," I answered, having to gasp for breath.

"That's Sam Bannock's dog, isn't it?" the yellowleg muttered. He was leaning one arm on a pine stick with the bark still on it. "What's it doing in Truckee?"

"You're choking me!" I cried out.

"Mean to," he breathed, and held me a little tighter. "Sam tell you to bring the dog?"

"Sam Bannock's in his grave!"

"Unless he jumped right back out of it. The actress lady's here, and there stands his dog. It's a regular re-

union. I believe I'd better keep an eye on both. Sam Bannock's likely to show up, big as life. But I can't let you run off and warn him, can I?"

For all I knew, he intended to wring my neck on the spot, but I didn't wait to find out. I kicked the pine branch out from under his arm, but he caught it. His weight shifted to his sore foot, and I could see his face tighten up with pain. Then he raised the stick in a fury to quilt me with it, and that was a mistake.

I didn't even see Jim Ugly start. Suddenly he was there under our feet, with his fangs bared and death in his throat.

The yellowleg dropped me and tried to fend off those lunging white teeth with the pine branch. There was an awful commotion, and I knew that Jim Ugly could bring him down. But then I came to my senses.

If folks took Jim Ugly to be a man-killer, they'd shoot him on the spot!

I saw him about to lunge again. I stepped in front and tried to wave him off.

"No! No! Back off! Stop!"

Jim Ugly grazed past my leg, and I jumped on him. I wrapped my arms around his hindquarters and held tight. His blood was up, and I thought he'd turn on me in a flash, but he didn't. I got him calmed down, and when I looked up, the yellowleg was gone.

I was close to tears. It was sheer fright, mostly, but it was also that Jim Ugly wasn't going to let a man take a stick to me. I never guessed he'd do that. I never guessed that he cared about me.

11

I Become
an Actor

We were both soaking wet when I got Jim Ugly over to the theater. The door was now locked, so we sat under the wooden awning and watched the rain.

"I'm obliged to you," I muttered.

He gave me one look with his sharply slanting wolf eyes, as if to say I was kind of pesky to have around but he was getting used to me. Then he returned to his own thoughts. I'd like to have held out my hand to see if he would nuzzle it. But I was afraid that he wouldn't, so I didn't. After a moment he moved off to be by himself and curled up with his tongue hanging out.

I decided to give the Arizona Girl back her seventy-five cents. For all I knew, the yellowleg had put Jim Ugly on his bounty list and was oiling up his Colt revolver. We'd better get out of town any way we could. There was bound to be a freight wagon leaving Truckee for somewhere, and maybe I could go along.

It had hardly stopped raining when a black buggy came along, glistening like a beetle, and out stepped William Tell and Miss Jenny.

When she saw Jim Ugly, her eyebrows rose in the air. "Look at that poor dog! He's soaked to the hide!"

So was I, but she didn't seem to notice that.

"He's all right," I said, and dug out the coins. "Here's the seventy-five cents back. I can't be in your play tonight."

"Can't?" Her hand went to her heart as if to stanch a mortal wound. "But you must! Who'll I get to play the role!"

"I don't know, miss."

"At this desperate hour! We'll have to cancel the performance!"

"I'm sorry," I said. "There's someone with a Colt

revolver apt to shoot my dog on sight."

"If he doesn't get taken by pneumonia first! Come inside."

William Tell had fished out a key to the door, and Miss Jenny led us down the aisle to the rear. Like a magician, she plucked her little dog from her coat and handed it to William Tell. She found a handful of rags, flung off her coat and hat, and went to work. She rubbed down Jim Ugly's fur as if she were polishing brass.

"Why would anyone want to shoot this glorious beast? He looks part wolf."

"He is," I replied softly.

That was enough to worry most folks, but it didn't seem to bother her.

"Anyone with a Colt in his hand will have to deal with me!"

William Tell spread a long arm, as if in introduction. "The Arizona markswoman. Rascals and ruffians, beware!"

She spared me a glance. "Of course you'll be in the performance tonight," she declared firmly. "You're an actor now. Frederick, the boy looks half drowned. Find him something dry to put on. And rehearse him in his part."

85

Frederick turned out to be William Tell and the Arizona Girl's husband. She said they'd keep Jim Ugly in the dressing room, and I agreed to keep the seventy-five cents.

The only clothes around that fit me were the knee breeches, white stockings, and blue jacket that William Tell's son wore in the play. So I wore them, while my own clothes hung up to dry near the potbellied stove.

Frederick showed me where one of the actors, playing a soldier, would grab me by the arm and lead me onstage. And once I had the apple balanced on my head, I was to say, "Father, Father, I fear not! Let the arrow find its mark!"

When night fell, the theater was lit, and William Tell himself went out front to sell tickets. The rain had stopped, but the roads would be mud. Miss Jenny introduced me to the other actors, who began making up their faces, and remarked grimly that we'd be playing to an empty house tonight, so don't be nervous.

I didn't feel nervous at all. I wasn't a real actor, like the rest of them, like my dad. I'd be hardly more than a piece of furniture standing with an apple on my head. And anyone could shout, "Father, Father, I fear not! Let the arrow find its mark!" It barely needed practicing.

Jim Ugly had curled up near the stove, hardly paying

attention to the goings-on, as if that was the way Dad trained him. He just about ignored the little dog, Pieface, and kept dozing off.

Mrs. William Tell, in a starchy white bonnet and petticoats a foot thick, stood at the peephole in the front curtain. She was squinting as if looking through a spyglass.

"We'll hold the curtain ten minutes," she said, clutching her snub-nosed dog. I wondered if she carried it onstage with her. "Muddy roads are bound to slow folks down, but here they come." And then she turned to me with a confident smile. "You won't let me down, will you? Ellis of the skunks has retired from an acting career, his mother tells me. Would you like to travel with us?" She didn't wait for me to answer. "Of course you would!"

She hurried off before I could open my mouth. After a moment I stood on my toes and put my eye to the peephole. Families came sauntering down the aisle and slipped off to chairs and benches. I saw kids waving or calling out to each other. And I saw Wilhelmina and Mr. Cornelius taking their places in a plush box along the left side of the theater.

There were other boxes, empty boxes, dark boxes, and I couldn't help imagining my dad slipping into one of them to watch the show. What a surprise he'd get seeing me up on the stage. Playacting. Like him.

Me! I had hated seeing him rush off to the theater. Plays seemed always to sprout wings, for they carried him off to other towns and cities. And he'd drop me off in one boarding school or another. Still, he always came back for me.

Frederick came rushing backstage with the money box and in no time at all transformed himself into William Tell with a flowing red beard. One of the Austrian soldiers in helmets, whose name was Abner, had his hands on a rope to lift the curtain as soon as he got the signal.

I took a last look through the peephole. A man in muddy boots came heavily down the aisle and fell into a seat. He stretched a sore foot in the aisle, and the yellow stripe down his pant leg was sharp as sunlight.

"Curtain!" called out Mrs. William Tell.

12

The
Message

I jumped out of the way. Abner pulled the rope, and the play began.

Seeing the yellowleg gave me something close to stage fright. I didn't want to go out there. He'd be sure to recognize me. And it was a clear fact he wouldn't let me slip off a second time.

He must have come looking for Wilhelmina, I thought. Was that what her message had said—to meet her here? I looked over at the box. She appeared as carefree as a lark.

I ought to run, I thought. But if I turned up missing, how would Miss Jenny pull off the apple-shooting scene? I reckoned they'd have to drop the curtain.

I stood in the wings, not knowing what to do. And there she was, right beside me. "You'll be jim-dandy," she said. "And the audience looks friendly. I don't see anyone with rotten eggs to throw. Recollect your lines?"

I nodded.

She shoved her dog into my hands. "Watch Pieface for me," she said, and walked onstage to a thunder of applause.

But suddenly I didn't remember my lines. What was I supposed to say? I imagined the soldier balancing the apple on my head and everyone waiting for me to speak. Say what? And all the while the yellowleg would be peering at me with his cold, hollow eyes.

I watched the stage and tried to calm myself. The story was something about a villain named Gessler. He wore a military cape and polished boots, and he'd hung his Austrian hat in a treetop. He commands all the Swiss mountain people to bow before it, to show respect for the Austrians, who had conquered them.

Mrs. William Tell, unseen by everyone, takes up a longbow and shoots the hat out of the tree. A shout of joy goes up, and everyone thinks it was Mr. William

Tell. The markswoman backs off into the wings.

She took her dog out of my hands and nuzzled it. And then she straightened the wig on my head. "You don't go on until the end of the act, but don't meander off. Remember—look fierce and defiant."

The wig! I must have broken into a huge smile. I'd forgot all about the wig I was wearing. I rushed from the wings to a dressing room mirror to peer at myself.

The wig sat like an overturned soup bowl on my head, pale as broomstraw and almost as stiff. I hardly recognized myself. How would the yellowleg know me?

I laughed out loud, and Jim Ugly opened one eye to look at me. And then he shut it again.

Onstage, Gessler was threatening William Tell with a horrible death. "Huntsman, I will free you on only one condition," snarled the villain, swirling his cloak. "Shoot an apple off the head of your son, and I will spare you!"

William Tell falls to his knees and clasps his fingers. "No! No! My dear little son! My hands may tremble!"

A few moments later the Austrian soldier, Abner, grabbed my arm and pulled me into the blinding glare of the footlights. And my lines came rushing back to me.

"Father, Father, I fear not!" I shouted. "Let the arrow find its mark!"

The actors seemed a little startled, especially Mr. Wil-

liam Tell, whose hand was shaking like a caught fish. I realized I had spoken my lines too early in the play.

Abner stationed me against a painted tree, behind the glass shield, and balanced a green apple on top of my wig.

Meanwhile, Mr. William Tell is trying to get up his courage by filling his throat out of a wineskin. A couple of villagers help him on his unsteady legs through the trees—and into the wings. Unseen by the soldiers, Mrs. William Tell, wearing a curly red beard, switches places with him. From where I stood I saw her hand him Pie-face as he went offstage and she came on.

"Father, Father," I said again, hoping to make up for getting it wrong the first time. "Take aim! I fear not!"

Across the stage Miss Jenny let fly with an arrow. I could hear it sing in over the top edge of the glass and pierce the apple. A shout went up from the mountain people and a snarl from Gessler. The curtain fell, and the theater rattled with applause.

I listened to the roar of approval and realized that a small bit of it had been for me.

"An auspicious beginning," Frederick said, handing me the little pug-faced dog to hold.

I put my eye to the peephole and watched the linger-ing applause. I liked the sound of it.

My gaze drifted to the yellowleg. His chair was empty. He had left. He didn't come storming backstage, so I reckoned he hadn't recognized me. I could breathe easier for a while.

The stage was being changed for the next act, with a painted lake and a canoe set in front of the trees. Miss Jenny lifted Pieface out of my arm. "You must be a natural-born actor," she told me. "You've already learned to fatten your part!" But she didn't seem at all mad that I'd almost doubled my lines.

The curtain rose, and Gessler goes back on his word. He has Mr. William Tell bound in chains and rowed to a terrible dungeon across the lake. But the huntsman escapes and swims in his chains to safety.

Only in the last act does Gessler swirl his cape for the last time. He lies in the center of the stage with an arrow in his chest, and his last breaths come wheezing out like a bagpipe. The curtain slowly fell to whistles and applause.

I thought I'd like to stay with the play for a while. It was like being inside a dream.

The curtain rose again so that the whole troupe could take a bow. The Arizona Girl dragged me out with her, hugging Pieface in her other arm. I didn't exactly bow, but I bent a little and glanced over the footlights.

Later, when Wilhelmina and Mr. Cornelius came backstage, she said, "That dreadful yellowleg won't be troubling us for a while."

"I intend to keep my eye peeled," I murmured.

She gave a reckless little laugh. "For D. D. Skeats? That unfortunate man! Remember the message you delivered? It said to meet me during the second act at that dead grandfather of a hollow cedar tree. I have no doubt the family of skunks made him quite unfit for human company."

13
A Scent for Jim Ugly

The train carried us west, winding and chuffing its way down the long mountainside. As I was a member of her theater troupe, Miss Jenny had bought my ticket and paid for Jim Ugly as well. I could have sat in a coach seat with the other actors, but I wasn't sure that I should leave Jim Ugly alone in the baggage car. So I rode there with him.

Around me stood the painted forest all rolled up, and the lake and moonlight folded away on hinges, and the rest of Switzerland packed away in theater trunks. But the make-believe of the night before was still aglow in my head.

And maybe my dad would wander into the theater some night and see me behind the footlights. Wig or not, I wouldn't fool him. He'd know me!

The train vanished into tunnels and clattered over high bridges. We reached the foothills and charged across the flatlands. Finally, panting like a winded dog, the engine paused in Roseville, and we got off.

Miss Jenny rushed the forest straight to the theater, for the trees had to be hung and the props set up for the evening performance.

Wilhelmina gave everyone a tearful good-bye, and she made me promise to call on her when we got to San Francisco. I was surprised to discover that Mr. Cornelius had decided to stay behind in Truckee.

But that night, when I gazed through the peephole, hoping to find my dad in a theater seat, I saw Wilhelmina. How was it possible to miss the train? She had been sitting in it!

After the show she hurried backstage to lavish praise on everyone's performance—even mine. "I *had* to see the play again. I'm simply enchanted, Jenny! But you must give Jake Bannock proper billing in small letters, at the very least. Otherwise he may scamper off like a squirrel. No actor can walk away from his name out front!"

We played Roseville for two days and Sacramento for five. My name was added in small letters on the lobby display. Wilhelmina turned up for every performance. It began to dawn on me that it wasn't enchantment that brought her to the theater every night.

She was counting on Dad to turn up. She was counting on me to flush him out of hiding. That's why she wanted my name out front!

Our last afternoon in Sacramento I was watching the steamboats in the river when a voice sounded like a rifle shot. "Jake!"

I didn't have to turn around. I could have picked out that voice in the center of a whirlwind. It was my cousin Aurora, all in black.

She threw her arms around me as if I were drowning and she meant to save my life. "You poor boy! Running off! I promised to look after you, Jake."

"I don't need looking after, Aurora," I said.

"Of course you do! Letting someone shoot an apple off your head! Are you crazy?"

"I'm not going back to Blowfly," I declared.

Her eyes lit on Jim Ugly. "I thought you chased that dog off," she said.

"I changed my mind."

"He's a sheep killer, Jake. You can't keep a dog like that. Not knowing what he's apt to go after next."

"I'm keeping him," I answered. "Did Axie come with you?"

"Someone had to stay behind to feed the chickens."

"You can tell him not to worry about the apple on my head, but I can't tell you how it's done."

She suddenly remembered her purse and began to paw through it.

"If that gentleman hadn't come back to Blowfly, I'd never have found you."

"What gentleman?"

"That Mr. Cornelius."

I was taken by huge surprise. "He went back to Blowfly? Why?"

"To say a few psalms at your papa's grave."

He's going to dig it up! I thought. Well, let him. And for all I knew, the pine box would turn out to be full of diamonds. It was the diamonds Mr. Cornelius had gone to pay his respects to.

"Ah, here it is," said Aurora, waving a gray envelope in the air. "It came the day you left, Jake. An old letter from your dad. It must have been lost in the mail!"

I took it out of her fingers, and my heart began to rush. I saw at once that the flap had been torn open.

"You won't mind that I read it, Jake," she said.

"You had no right, Aurora."

"Of course I didn't. But he might have said something important."

"About the diamonds, you mean."

"What I mean is, how could a man write a letter from the other side of the grave, Jake? No, it was just slow in getting to us. He got the date wrong."

The top of the letter was dated more'n a week before. Aurora just wasn't able to see what was right in front of her eyes. She had watched a pine box lowered into the ground, and that was that, and nothing was going to shake what she saw in front of her eyes. *But, Aurora, if the date was right, my dad had to be alive!*

I didn't say it aloud. And for an instant I thought he must be sending for me. But Aurora would have said something. I looked for a return address, but my dad had left that blank. And he wasn't careless enough to leave a postmark you could read. He'd had the stamp canceled by hand.

> *My Dear Jake—It was not my intention to vanish without seeing you first. But I have come to expect the unexpected, and it became prudent to make a sudden stage exit. It will be better for you, and safer for me, if my whereabouts remain*

unknown. Say nothing and burn this letter,
keeping only the fatherly embrace and affection so
warmly enclosed. Your loving dad.

There was something in the letter that didn't match up, and I wanted to read it again. But not with Aurora standing there. I told her I was sorry she had come so far to get me, but Miss Jenny, the Arizona Girl, needed me in the show, and I couldn't leave. I said I'd get her in free of charge if she wanted to see the show tonight, and she finally left me to shop for some hat feathers.

I sat on the wharf and read the letter again. It came to me in a rush what was wrong. Dad hadn't so much as hinted at the fakery at the burying ground. There was nothing about act one, scene three of *The Huddlestone Ghost.*

It hit me like a thunderclap. He didn't know. I was positive of it. He didn't know Axie had pretended he was in the pine box six feet under!

I felt a tremendous lightness almost lift me off my feet. Dad thought he was only making another stage exit! He hadn't a notion I had grieved for him. It wasn't his fault!

I held out the letter before Jim Ugly's nose.

"You know that scent, don't you?" I said, grinning. "Take a good breath of it. And we might as well start looking in Sacramento."

14

The Man
on the
Trolley

I bought a long rope to put around Jim Ugly's neck
so he wouldn't leave me in his dust. I led him from
one theater to another, and his wet nose cut through the
air like a scythe. I walked him back along the train station. We covered the wharf, for my dad might have
taken a steamboat downriver. But there wasn't a trace
of him in the air anywhere.

Mrs. William Tell moved on to Oakland, and the second night there the yellowleg turned up big as life in the

audience. He must have aired out considerably, and he didn't appear to need a stick to lean on. But how had he found me? The way his eyes bore into me when I was onstage, it was clear he now knew who I was. I began to wonder if Mr. Cornelius might have told him I was with the play. But why would Mr. Cornelius do a spiteful thing like that?

The yellowleg sat like a waiting spider. He never smiled, he never laughed, and he never applauded.

He was waiting for my dad to turn up, I thought, the same as Wilhelmina.

In the daytimes I kept an eye out for them both and worked Jim Ugly around the theaters and the hotels. They couldn't have known what he was casting for, I thought. He appeared to be nothing but a dog following his nose.

Suddenly he almost jerked my arm off. We were on the wide Oakland wharf where the train tracks ended and the ferryboats docked. Jim Ugly danced in a sudden circle, his nose rising as if he'd lost the scent. But he caught it again, and we went flying through the sea gulls toward the ferry to San Francisco.

"Good dog!" I exclaimed, throwing my arms around his furry shoulders. "Jim Ugly, you're a wonder!"

I gazed across the bay at the windows of San Francisco, flashing in the pink morning sun. Dad was bound to be there, I thought. Not four miles away! He appeared to have got off the train at the end of the line in Oakland and caught the ferry to San Francisco.

I hurried to buy a ticket, and they let Jim Ugly ride free. After a while the ferryboat gave out a deep blast of its whistle, the engine began to thump, and we headed into open water. It couldn't have taken more than twenty minutes to cross the bay, but it seemed an eternity.

We stood up front in the wind, and I watched a couple of sea lions following close beside the boat as if they'd been taught to heel. Before long I could read the time on the clock set high in the tower of the ferry building in San Francisco. It was not yet ten-thirty. I had hours of time before I had to get back for the night's performance.

The nose of the ferry bumped into the splintered timbers of the ferry slip, and Jim Ugly and I were about the first off.

On the broad Embarcadero we slipped through the comings of freight wagons and goings of hotel carriages. There was a dusty hubbub all along the wharves. But once we reached Market Street, Jim Ugly appeared lost. The scent had vanished. We floundered about for a while, and then I led him back into the Embarcadero hubbub to start again.

And I caught sight of the yellowleg.

I hadn't seen him following me! I hadn't seen him slip aboard the ferryboat. But there he stood, a brown derby on his head, angrily waving off peddlers and newsboys.

I looked away in a hurry. I didn't want him to know I had seen him. Just then Jim Ugly caught the scent again near one of the carriages for hire. I gave his rope a sharp tug away.

"No!" I whispered. "This way."

I almost had to drag him along. I couldn't let him track my dad now—not with D. D. Skeats's eyes following us.

We turned a corner and turned another. We wound our way up a hill with cobbled streets and wound our way down the other side. Let the yellowleg think what he liked about the run I was leading him on. As soon as I could, I'd head back to Oakland.

Down among the warehouses and brick buildings I had only to wait in front of a glass window to see the yellow stripe down his leg amble into view.

Jim Ugly couldn't seem to understand what was wrong with me. He kept fighting the rope. Every so often he'd give me an impatient glance with his slanted eyes.

But when I turned a corner, he turned a corner.

And it happened that suddenly. I turned a corner and saw a thin man in a soft-brimmed hat step into a trolley car. He wore a brown linen duster down to his ankles, and the collar was thrown up around his neck.

It was Sam Bannock.

It was my dad.

I almost burst to keep from yelling out. He hadn't seen me, and I wanted to run for the trolley. But I froze.

The yellowleg had come into view. I could see him reflected in the window.

The trolley clanged its bell and started forward. I felt as if I'd been split by lightning. But I managed to take another loop on Jim Ugly's rope. He might catch a fresh scent and go bolting down the tracks.

I turned him roughly away to cross the street.

"Come along!" I said bitterly. "Do what I say!"

I couldn't keep the tears out of my eyes. But the yellowleg couldn't see them, and he'd never know Sam Bannock was in the trolley clattering away down the street.

At least I knew that my father was in town. I'd be back.

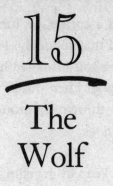

15

The Wolf

I could hardly keep my mind on being the son of William Tell that night. But I managed to keep the apple balanced on my head and to say my lines.

I had just finished my part and stepped offstage when I heard a sudden growl from the dressing room. I knew it was Jim Ugly, and I knew something was wrong.

I flew down the steps. I don't know why Mr. William Tell, offstage, wasn't holding Miss Jenny's snub-nosed dog. But he wasn't. Jim Ugly had appeared to tolerate

Pieface fine, and I'd even seen him try to play with her.

When I reached the dressing room, he had Pieface between his jaws. My skin went prickly. It was the timber wolf in Jim Ugly that looked back at me. He'd changed as suddenly as a weather vane in a contrary gust of wind.

In another second he might tighten his jaws and break Pieface's neck. The attack must have come so suddenly that the small dog was too astonished even to yelp.

"Jim Ugly," I said softly, holding my voice as firm as it would come out. "Stop. Don't move. Listen to me. Jim Ugly, I'm coming close."

I put my fingers out, slow and steady. I knew I had to jam my hand into his mouth. "Easy. Hold still." I looked at his sharply pointing ears, my heart banging away. "Hold still. Hold still."

I touched Pieface's fur. She gave me a puzzled flash of her eyes. If she squealed, I knew that Jim Ugly's jaws would snap together like a trap. But she was so accustomed to being passed from one actor to another that she hadn't panicked. She appeared to be in a state of frozen amazement.

"Let me take the dog," I said hoarsely. And I worked my fingers between Jim Ugly's teeth.

He couldn't bite down now without getting both of

us. And I didn't think he'd do that to me. I smiled a little.

"Good dog, Jim Ugly."

His teeth seemed to tremble. He didn't want to back down. But he did. He let me take Pieface out of his mouth.

"Thank you," I said, and suddenly I knew for a certainty that Jim Ugly was my dog. "Thank you, Amigo."

16

I Let
Jim Ugly
Loose

The Swiss mountainside was packed and loaded
aboard the ferry. We were to play for three weeks
at Mr. Cornelius's own Mazeppa Theater on Geary
Street.

I was ready for San Francisco. I had a note carefully
written out, warning my father not to come anywhere
close—that D. D. Skeats was sticking to me like a tick,
and Wilhelmina was, too.

I made a dog collar out of rope and tied my note

around it with about a dozen loops of twine. At the crack of dawn I returned to Sansome Street, a block from where I'd watched my dad catch the trolley.

I dropped to my knees and tightened my arms around Jim Ugly's thick, furry neck. "I have to turn you loose," I said. "You can trail Dad on your own. Find him, Amigo."

I pulled out my father's own letter to give him a fresh sniff of it. "Get going. Go on, now. Sashay out of here."

In hardly any time at all he was casting for the scent. His fur seemed to bristle with excitement. He came back to me once, brushing against my leg, and looked up at me as if to make sure I wasn't trying to drive him away again.

"You don't see me pitching any rocks at you, do you? Don't be so touchy! Find him, Amigo!"

I watched him sniff along the storefronts. Suddenly he whipped around the corner and was gone from sight. I took a deep breath and turned away. I didn't think I'd call him Jim Ugly anymore. Once he found my dad, I figured he'd turn into Sam Bannock's one-man dog again.

But maybe he wouldn't. I began to walk and wondered how soon I'd see him again.

□   □   □

The Mazeppa Theater was upstairs over a brownstone horse barn. There were great stretches of empty chairs at the performance that night. And those who came appeared mostly to have forgot their umbrellas and ducked in to escape the wet, dripping fog.

There was a soft rattle of applause when the curtain rose and the play began. The actors had to speak up against the foghorns, calling out from the bay like infernal bullfrogs.

I waited in the wings for my entrance. Miss Jenny thrust Pieface into my arms to go onstage and lifted her out again the moment she bounded offstage. She didn't know that Amigo had come close to killing her little dog. I didn't imagine the wildness could ever be entirely trained out of Amigo. And that suited me fine. If every so often the ghost of a wolf came leaping out of him, the world would just have to stand back for a moment. He was entitled to be what he was.

I was dimly aware of the Austrian soldier coming in his polished steel helmet to take my arm and lead me onstage. I wondered what had happened to Abner, who was usually costumed for the part. This actor was taller, with longer arms and thinner fingers around my arm.

We were out in front of the footlights before I happened to glance into his face.

I saw my father. He appeared high, mighty, and big as all creation!

"Dad!"

He gave me a wink with his upstage eye. He shielded me from the audience as he balanced the apple on my head.

"If you're going to be an actor, Jake, don't embarrass the play with gawkish dialogue of your own. Hold still."

"But they're out there—all of them," I muttered, hardly letting my lips move.

"That will be convenient."

It was time to deliver my line, and I remembered to look fierce and defiant. "Father, Father, fear not! Let the arrow find its mark!"

To my surprise, the Austrian soldier in the polished steel helmet began to speak.

"O huntsman, stay your hand a moment!" said my father in his rich stage voice. "How like a tiny gem sits the apple—would you like a larger target? Such gems I have in abundance. You will find me gracious in these negotiations. If not, proceed."

I don't know what Miss Jenny thought of the Austrian soldier suddenly taking it into his head to burst into dialogue. It was clear to me that Dad was talking directly to the audience. He was telling the yellowleg huntsman to hold his fire until they could talk. Gems? The diamonds!

The Arizona Girl shot the apple off my head, and I rushed offstage into my father's embrace.

Then he fixed me with his playful actor's eyes. "What's this, Jake? A second thespian in the family! We must seek out better material to display your talents. Perhaps Wilhelmina can help. You've met her, of course."

"Yes."

"Do you like her?"

"I think so," I said.

"I think she means to have me horsewhipped!"

He laughed and dismissed the matter with a toss of his hand. We walked downstairs to the dressing room, where Amigo was curled up waiting. Dad petted him, and I petted him.

"Your dog's got a fine nose," I said softly. I realized that I'd only borrowed Amigo for a while.

"Yes."

"He knew right off you weren't in the graveyard."

"Axie meant well," he said with a flash of anger. "He thought it would throw off D. D. Skeats forever to put on that funeral. But he should have spared you, Jake. He should have told you."

When the curtain fell on the last act, the theater emptied. But I saw Wilhelmina and Mr. Cornelius in one of the private boxes and, across the theater, D. D. Skeats sitting with his derby hat on his lap.

And in the back I saw Axie.

The footlights were still ablaze when my father stepped in front of the curtain.

"Cornelius, you've encouraged that yellow-legged nitwit to fire lead at me and to otherwise disturb the peace of my family. I retire from the game. You win. The gems are yours. I will lead you to them tomorrow."

"None of your actor's tricks!" Mr. Cornelius shouted. "That funeral didn't fool us!"

"On my word as an actor, no actor's tricks," replied my father. He seemed to be enjoying himself in front of the footlights, as if he were writing a play for himself on the spot.

"The diamonds were not in the coffin!" Mr. Cornelius cried out scornfully.

"They've been moved. Tomorrow at seven in the morning we will assemble at the ferry building for something of a journey. Agreed?"

"Agreed," said Mr. Cornelius.

"And you, Wilhelmina?"

"Yes," she said airily. "Let's do fetch the diamonds, Sam—and then I'll have you horsewhipped! I may even do it myself!"

17

Blowfly

We reached Smoketree Junction at four twenty-three the next afternoon. Dad had wired ahead to have burros waiting at the train depot.

"Do you expect me to ride one of those things?" Wilhelmina protested.

"Suit yourself, Willy," my dad replied. "The diamond mine can't be more than ten miles off. You're free to walk."

"What diamond mine?" Wilhelmina exclaimed with sudden awe.

"Didn't our friend Cornelius tell you?" my dad replied. "He has not been entirely forthcoming, has he? A diamond mine, indeed. He came into possession of one only to misplace it."

"How could *anyone* misplace a diamond mine?"

"It was remarkably careless," my dad said.

Mr. Cornelius stood with his jaw shut tight as an oyster. The yellowleg stood behind him like an unhappy shadow.

When everyone was seated on burros, my dad snapped out three white handkerchiefs. "You will understand if I insist that you be blindfolded. Only Axie here knows the exact location of the diamond mine, and Axie is a man of secrets. Here you are. Blindfolds of the finest linen."

"Me, too?" asked Wilhelmina.

"Most certainly you."

"But no woman can look fetching in a blindfold. Not even Justice in all those marble statues."

And so we set out for Blowfly, with Amigo racing on ahead of us. A hot desert wind had come up, blowing sand in our faces, and Wilhelmina stopped complaining about the blindfold and the burro. I think all her protesting was just to keep herself in my father's eye.

And I was sure he had wired for burros instead of

horses because it took the frills out of Mr. Cornelius to be led along on such a backwoodsy little animal.

Before long, Dad led the party off the road and took us wandering in great loops and switchbacks. He'd have them so confused they wouldn't be able to find their noses without a compass.

Axie hadn't said a word to me, even in San Francisco. But I found him pulling up beside me.

"I don't blame you for being mad," he said.

I just looked straight ahead.

"It pained me to see you grieving, Jake. It was hard to lie to you. But I had to do things that way. It might save your pa's life with that bounty hunter breathing so close. I didn't think you'd be able to act up the tears if you knew the pine box was only full of ice. And then Mr. Cornelius and the lady turned up, and I figured I better not tell you yet."

"I'm not mad at you, Axie. I reckon you had to do it the way you did."

"I'm obliged, Jake."

I took a breath and hoped to let the subject drop away. "Did Aurora find feathers for her hat in Sacramento?" I asked.

"Lots of 'em. But why she needs feathers in her hat to feed chickens in Blowfly I'll never know."

He fell back to lead the pack for a while, and I rode side by side with my father.

"Sam!" Wilhelmina yelled out. "Are you still there? How do I know you won't abandon us to perish in this savage, godforsaken desert?"

"I wouldn't do that, Willy."

"You abandoned me once before! At the wedding chapel! And I'll horsewhip you for it!"

He turned his glance my way and mumbled, " 'Heck has no fury like a woman scorned,' as the poet said. Or did he use stronger language?"

"All my friends were there, Sam! I was standing in so much white lace I looked like an Alps mountaintop. There was enough rice to plant China!"

I said, "You could have told me you were going to get married again."

"She's not much like your mother, is she, Jake?"

"No, sir."

"I figured it might be easier to catch you by surprise. Done and over with."

"But I like her," I said.

I caught his glance. He seemed pleased.

We were zigzagging all over the place but heading in the general direction of Blowfly. Amigo had got out of sight, and Dad gave him a whistle. "Come here, Amigo!"

I was surprised that Amigo didn't come at the sound of his voice.

"Amigo!" I called. "Here!"

He burst out of the dust and came bounding up on his big paws and circled me. I looked at Dad. "I guess he didn't hear you," I said.

"He heard me, all right," my dad said, and thought for a moment. "Jake, I think you've got yourself a dog."

I broke out in a smile. Jim Ugly was mine. Amigo was mine. I had myself a dog.

We were swinging back toward the road. Finally I asked, "Is there really a diamond mine out here? In Blowfly?"

"You'll see for yourself," he said with a narrow grin. And then, speaking softly, he told me what had happened. He had Amigo with him in Grass Valley, where Mr. Cornelius had rented the theater and hired him to act in *The Huddlestone Ghost*. Grass Valley was in the High Sierras, and Axie had come up to see him in the play. My dad decided to show him what a powerful nose Amigo had for tracking.

"I found an old army cap someone had discarded behind the hotel. Amigo tracked it about four miles up a mountainside to a jumble of crevices and fallen rocks. We came upon a yellowleg sergeant planting diamonds as if they were corn seed. And there stood Cornelius in leather boots telling him what to do. They were 'salting' a mine with diamonds. He could sell shares in it and swindle people out of millions of dollars."

"Were they *real* diamonds?" I asked.

"Real enough, Jake. After they left, Axie and I picked out all the stones we could find with our pocketknives. We must have collected thirty or forty pounds of rough, sparkling diamonds. I knew that Cornelius wouldn't let millions of dollars' worth of gems sit unattended. They were most certainly junk diamonds."

"Junk diamonds?"

"Expensive trash. The sort of diamonds that end up in drill bits and cheap watches. I'd even found one discarded fragment with a facet cut into it. After my performance that night I told Cornelius I had his diamonds.

" 'That diamond mine of yours not only grows diamonds, it cuts them, too!' I said, throwing down the stone with the facet.

"He went red in the face, of course. He offered to make me a partner. I declined. He said he had put up his interest in the Mazeppa Theater to raise money to buy the trash diamonds. He had even used Wilhelmina's money. She was bound to lose everything if she didn't help him. He floated the rumor among my fellow actors that someone had put a bounty on my head. I began to feel like a fly in a roomful of fly swatters. The next thing I knew D. D. Skeats was taking potshots at me. Right from the beginning Cornelius has been giving him orders. I chose to disappear."

"I'll bet that's why you didn't show up for your own wedding!" I blurted out.

"That pestiferous yellowleg is such a poor shot he'd more likely have hit Wilhelmina. I thought we'd be safe here and arranged for the diamonds to be sent in a cheap coffin to Smoketree Junction. When Axie and I went to pick it up, I saw Cornelius's hired man step off the train. The yellowleg was getting too close for comfort. I had to leave you behind without a word. I left the coffin with Axie."

"Mr. Cornelius dug it up. The box was empty."

"Axie is a man of the finest caution," my dad said. "Have you any notion what he did with the diamonds?"

I shook my head.

My dad leaned closer and lowered his voice to a bemused whisper.

"He mixed them with chicken mash and fed them to his hens. That herd of chickens, Jake, is a diamond mine on legs. Those hens are running around with gems in their craws!"

I glanced back at Axie, who gave me a finger flick of his hat as if he knew exactly what we were talking about. And maybe he did.

If we were only going to Axie's chicken barn in Blowfly, I didn't see any reason to blindfold everybody. "Pure theater," my dad explained grandly. "Look at them trailing one after the other. It's perfect staging! If you're going to be an actor, Jake, you must develop a sense of theater."

A distant yell caught our ears. It was Aurora in her buggy over on the road. She turned off and spun across the trickling creek bed toward us.

Axie came forward, handing the lead burro's reins to Dad. He squinted his eyes at Aurora.

"What are you doing here?" she yelled out. "Axie! How come you didn't let me know you were back?"

Axie seemed alarmed to find Aurora all dressed up, with feathers in her hat and suitcases piled in the buggy.

The wind was with her, and she reached us in a cloud of dust.

"Aurora," Axie said softly. "Where are you going?"

"Axie, I can't listen to one more chicken cackle! I don't want to homestead out here. I want to homestead in the city, and that's where you'll find me."

"Did you water the chickens?" Axie asked.

"I'm through watering chickens!"

"Who's taking care of them?"

"They'll have to take care of themselves. I swear you worry more about those chickens than you do me. I opened the barn door wide yesterday morning and chased the lot of them out."

"Aurora," Axie murmured. It was a sound of pure pain.

But my dad took it all in with a grin. "Those hens are gone, Aurora? Let loose? On the run?" He swung a leg over the burro and planted his legs on the ground. "Gentlemen and lady, take off your blindfolds. You've heard this startling news. The Great Tumbleweed Diamond Mine is on the march once more! Your gems, Cornelius, are in the gizzards of the dispossessed poultry. I have no doubt that chicken hawks and coyotes have taken their toll, and jackrabbits have chased the rest. I'm afraid you'll have hundreds of square miles of desert to search. It's falling dark, but make haste. Look there! I believe there's a rooster in that cactus patch. With luck you may catch enough cackling gemstones to make a gaudy little necklace."

"I'm ruined!" Mr. Cornelius cried out, and his weeping willow eyebrows rose as if blown in a sudden storm.

Aurora fainted dead away when she learned she'd had enough diamonds in the barn to hang the sky at night, only to turn them loose.

Mr. Cornelius pleaded for compass directions to the train station in Smoketree Junction. He whipped his burro, and D. D. Skeats followed like a dusty vulture with fading yellow stripes down his legs. "I want my pay!" he bellowed at Mr. Cornelius's back. "I cornered Bannock for you. I want the bounty money."

"Idiot! There was no bounty money!"

It looked as if the yellowleg was going to stick to Mr. Cornelius like a cocklebur.

It was almost a week before we returned to San Francisco, all of us. The Arizona Girl had been able to replace me easily enough in San Francisco, but she said I could have the job back anytime I wanted.

Wilhelmina seemed greatly subdued. She never once spoke of losing her savings to Cornelius and his junk diamonds. She hadn't known the yellowleg took his orders from Mr. Cornelius. "He might have killed you, Sam! And to think I was trying to help that contemptible Cornelius!" she wailed, dabbing at her nose with a handkerchief as lacy as a handful of air.

And then one day she was laughing again and said she guessed she wouldn't horsewhip my father after all.

"Unless you stand me up again in all that white lace and rice." I kind of liked the idea of my dad marrying her.

I saw the wolf come out in Amigo only once during those days. Wilhelmina had sent me on an errand to the Palace Hotel on Market Street, and I'd tied Amigo outside to a lamppost. When I returned, he'd chewed the rope through. He was sitting beside it, his yellow eyes flaring up like heat lightning. I nodded to him, respectfully, and said, "Hello, Jim Ugly."